DECORATIVE STENCI
FOR INTERIOR DESIGN

DECORATIVE STENCILS FOR INTERIOR DESIGN

Over 150 stencil motifs from classic architectural periods

Magie M. Maule

STUDIO
VISTA

To my dear friend Jonathan Phillips
for much shared laughter and real talk.

First published in the United Kingdom in 1991

Studio Vista
Villiers House
41/47 Strand
London WC2N 5JE

A Cassell imprint
by arrangement with CollinsAngus&Robertson Publishers Pty Limited,
Sydney, Australia

First published in Australia in 1991 by
CollinsAngus & Robertson Publishers Pty Limited
A division of HarperCollinsPublishers (Australia) Pty Limited
4 Eden Park, 31 Waterloo Road, North Ryde, NSW 2113, Australia

British Library Cataloguing in Publication Data
Maule, Magie
Decorative stencils.
1. Residences. Interiors. Decoration
I. Title
747.88

ISBN 0-289-80051-X

Typeset in Australia
Printed and bound in Australia by Griffin Press

CONTENTS

INTRODUCTION

When writing this book, I had a two-fold purpose in mind: to summarise particular design periods into their essential style elements and to offer designs in stencil form which a beginner could use to create original and stunning effects. It is a very personal collection of designs; but I have tried to pass on motifs that seemed to me to capture the essence of a particular period.

Stencilling has become one of the most popular forms of home decoration. Part of this revival in the art of stencilling has been due to a renewed appreciation of the skills of the craftsman — an appreciation of the homemade as opposed to the machine-made. Stencilling is also one of the easiest of crafts to take up and provides instant results. The artistic amateur can make a very good job of a stencilled room or piece of furniture by using a little patience and care in following instructions.

For those of you restoring and renovating houses, this book provides a range of traditional borders and motifs to provide authentic historical flavour. However, there are also many designs that will allow your imagination free rein to create a totally individual look.

Before listing the sources from which these designs have been drawn, I have outlined some basic facts about stencilling for the first-time stenciller.

A stencil can be a piece of cardboard (stencil board), plastic (mylar) or metal (usually brass) into which you cut holes to form a design. Paint is brushed or sprayed through these holes to create the decorative pattern. The holes are held together by bridges, or ties, of material. In some fine Japanese stencils they may be held together by human hair or fine silk. The ties are arranged to make the stencil strong and also outline or highlight the design because the areas where the ties or bridges occur do not print and so retain the background colour. A good stencil design integrates the ties so that they accentuate and enhance the motif. You can use one stencil to make as many repeats of the design as you wish, so for the small amount of initial effort required in cutting your stencil you are rewarded by being able to decorate large areas very quickly.

Stencilling is one of the most ancient and enduring art forms. Probably the first stencillers were Palaeolithic cave-dwellers who used the hand as a stencil and pushed paint between the fingers and around the outline. There is also evidence that stencilling was used by the Egyptians on tomb walls and in coffin decorations. Stencils were also used in early Chinese textiles and sacred texts.

During the Middle Ages and continuing into the Renaissance, stencilling was used extensively for wall decorations and for the decorative gold background in oil paintings, fabric and leather work.

During the seventeenth, eighteenth and nineteenth centuries stencils were used in a greater variety of ways — as 'drop-in' colour to block prints, wall hangings, wallpapers, playing cards, religious books and furniture decoration. At this time stencilling also became a popular alternative to expensive wallpaper for wall decoration with journeymen travelling around towns and villages offering their stencilling services.[1] Stencilling became particularly popular in the United States in the nineteenth century, having been brought to the new world by German and Scandinavian immigrants. Stencils were used both on walls and floors and often to decorate the entire surface.[2]

It is the 'repeating' quality of stencils that makes them so useful. Stencils were used extensively when speed, quantity and economy were required. Stencils were not superseded until the Industrial Revolution saw hand work give way to machines. Stencilling then became too costly to use.

This book provides designs from the whole history of Western art; from ancient Greece and Rome through to the Renaissance, Baroque and Rococo periods of the fifteenth, sixteenth and seventeenth centuries. There are also more modern designs including patterns from the Victorian and Art Nouveau periods and finally Art Deco designs that bring us into the twentieth century. There is also a section on Folk Art which is probably timeless in style, although the particular designs I have chosen are from the seventeenth, eighteenth and nineteenth centuries.

I have provided a brief summary of the main stylistic features and concerns of each of these periods, together with suggested colours to use. However this is of a very general nature as this book is intended as an overview and not a history of art. If you are interested in knowing more about particular periods discussed, there is a list of further reading at the end of the introduction. I have tried to keep technical terms to a minimum but where this has been unavoidable the glossary at the back of the book may be of some help.

I am sure you will find stencilling an immensely enjoyable and rewarding craft, and hope that my designs will help you to create a unique and beautiful room you will be proud of.

GETTING STARTED

Read the following instructions carefully before you start stencilling. The stencils in this book have been designed so that all you need do is photocopy the chosen design, trace it onto a stencil board, cut out all the black areas and brush paint through the holes you make — that is where your colour will appear.

Most of the designs in this book are stencilled in one colour. If you would like to use more than one colour, instructions are provided on page 11.

Some of the stencil designs are very simple, others are a bit more time consuming to cut. However, I think you will find that these more complex designs are well worth the extra effort.

Make sure your stencils are large enough to work with easily and are in good proportion to the area you are working on — whether it be walls, floors, furniture or fabric. Some designs may need to be enlarged using a photocopier.

TRACING YOUR STENCIL

Materials

Carbon paper
Oiled stencil board or acetate sheet[3]
Sharp pencil or pen

The traditional method is to trace the design onto the tracing paper from the book, and work from that, but if you have enlarged your design on a photocopier, you can draw directly around that.

First, place your tracing, or enlarged photocopy on top of a piece of carbon paper, underneath which is the stencil board or acetate — that makes a three-layer sandwich.

Next, press firmly with your sharp pencil around all the outlines, pressing down through the carbon paper onto the stencil board or acetate, so that you transfer the design via the carbon onto the stencil.

The stencil board should have straight edges and the carbon paper and photocopy be placed at right angles to it and secured with drawing pins to prevent movement.

The stencil board should be at least 5 cm (2 in) larger than the design (on all sides) to leave a border to prevent paint from getting onto the background accidentally.

CUTTING YOUR STENCIL

Materials

Sharp knife or surgeon's scalpel (always kept stuck into a cork for safety)
Cutting board (I always use the cardboard backs of my tracing pads — but you can use a sheet of metal, or glass plate with the edges cornered with sticky tape)
Sticky tape (insulating tape for glass edges)
Needles (to poke out small circles, if required)
Fine sandpaper (to sand down projections on the back of the stencil board if you have poked out holes with your needle)
Stencil board with design drawn on it

Place the stencil on the cutting board, holding the knife edge at an angle of 45 degrees as you cut. Cut out all the outlined areas and remove the pieces released. Work from the smallest areas to the largest to prevent weakening the bridges or ties — the thin strips of material that separate the holes and hold the stencil together. Take care with corners. If you overshoot the outline you might cut through 'bridges'; if you do this, mend the cut with sticky tape on both sides for strength.

Small areas and holes can be poked out with needles, and the rough bits on the back of the stencil caused by this must be fine sanded to keep the stencil flat when printing. When all the areas to be removed have been cut out, your stencil is finished and ready to print.

APPLYING YOUR STENCIL

PAINT

Always use oil-based paint when painting floors, wood or furniture. You can use acrylics or other paints on walls if you like, but I almost always stick to oils. Artists' oil paints are fine, or you can use special stencilling paints if available.

Mix the oil paint with turps in a flat-bottomed container, like an old saucer or plate, until you have a thin cream with no lumps. If you are using more than 250 ml (9 fl oz) it should be strained through an old stocking to make sure there are no 'bits' in the mixture (particularly if you are using paint from a pot which has been used before) because paint brushes often have dust or grit in them which gets transferred to the container.

BRUSHES

A few different sized stencil brushes may be required depending on the kind of stencilling you are doing.

For general work one fine, two medium and one large should be enough. A brush for each colour, all of the same size, is the rule, because you can't wash out your brush until the end of the work (turps in the brush would thin out the next lot of paint and make it smudge the work around the edges). To clean your brushes just wipe them on an old cloth to remove surplus paint. There can be a very small amount of turps on the rag.

You can stencil without a brush by using an air brush or spray can; but if you do this you will need to protect the surroundings with larger areas of masking tape and newspaper as spray paint can drift a long way from the paint site. Wear a mask, hat and overalls when spraying.

HOW TO PAINT WITH A STENCIL BRUSH

Stencilling is not like conventional painting where the brush is moved from side to side. A stencil brush is always held like a pen between thumb, index and second fingers, not like a conventional brush. The flat cut-off bristles on a stencil brush are held parallel to the printing surface and the painting motion is one of tapping through the stencil with the loaded brush, lifting the brush off cleanly each time, but tapping rapidly and making sure that you tap from the edges to the centre of each opening in the stencil to stop paint creeping under the stencil and smudging the print. This tapping motion is called *pouncing*.

Once your paint is mixed you can try out your first stencil on paper. Dip your brush a little into the paint, covering only the tips of the bristles. Now tap onto a piece of newspaper. Keep tapping in several places till a lot of the paint is off the brush. When you think there is hardly any paint on it, you can start tapping your brush or *pouncing* through the design using as little paint as possible. This ensures that the design has a good crisp edge and that it dries quickly.

STENCILLING ON DIFFERENT SURFACES

As a general rule, before you start stencilling you should prepare the surface. Make sure that all surfaces are finely sanded, brushed free of all dust and free from grease. Holes and faults should be filled a little high and then sanded back flat. Furniture and painted wooden surfaces in good condition can be washed down with sugar soap or detergent. Any slightly irregular or shiny surfaces should be sanded back with water and 'wet and dry' paper using small circular movements. This produces a matt surface that takes paint easily.

Materials

Oil paint
Stencil brushes (small, medium or large depending on the work involved)
Spray mount and solvent
Chalk, chalk-liners and a plumb bob for walls
Set square
Pencil
Masking tape
Newspaper
Old rags
Old saucer or plate
Turpentine
Sheet of drawing paper
Scissors

WALLS

When stencilling walls, you will probably be stencilling repeating borders, spot designs where motifs are regularly placed but not connected, or a repeating, all-over design.

Whichever pattern you are doing, the structure of the design should be mapped out in chalk which can then be rubbed off easily afterwards.

First use your plumb bob to establish your true uprights (straight vertical lines) by hanging it from the ceiling and letting it swing until it comes to rest. The plumb bob string should be covered with chalk by running your chalk up and down the string until it is well coated. Hold the string of the bob at top and bottom against the wall (you will need two people) then pull out the string in the middle towards you, like plucking a guitar string, and let it flick against the wall — it will leave a perfectly straight chalk line from which you can measure all other vertical and horizontal lines using a set square. Map out the geometric structure that you require for all-over repeats, for example, so that you will know where every stencil falls in squares, diamonds, bands, and so on.

If you are doing a line of stencils you will need to know where to position your second, third, and subsequent stencils in relation to the first. On acrylic this is easy. Place your cut out stencil next to the original design. Decide what space there will be between them and make knicks or large dots at two or three places on the acrylic; when you make the next stencil design, you will always place these dots or knicks in the same spot in relation to the previous print (you will have to wait for the previous stencil to dry, otherwise you will pick up paint on your stencil board).

On stencil board that is not transparent, punch out small holes that you can see through, or use knicks in the edge of the stencil, so that you always get the same piece of the previous stencil showing through the hole. This procedure ensures that the

Colour 1

Colour 2

Colour 3

This step-by-step stencil of a Greek anthemion indicates how separate colours build into a complete design.

If you want to use different colours on the one stencil, identify the areas that will appear in each colour. Some of the stencil designs in this book have been printed in different shades of grey as a guide to where different colours can be used.

Work with one colour at a time, masking off any spaces on the stencil that you don't want printed in that particular colour. Once you print the first colour, cover all those spaces on the stencil with masking tape and print your next colour, and so on for each new colour.

Small lines such as facial features will need to be painted separately by hand.

repeats are evenly spaced. Try this system on clean paper before you start on the walls.

To stencil walls, stick the stencil to the wall with masking tape (not sticky tape) or spray the back of the stencil with spray mount following directions for its use on the back of the can. When you have painted your design through your stencil it must be carefully removed and, for repeats, re-stuck down for the next stencil.

If you use spray mount, keep the stencil on a dry, shiny surface to avoid it picking up dust or grit, or if you are using stencil board, keep your stencil on clean newspaper and wipe off any surplus paint now and then to avoid paint build up. You can clean your stencil properly with turps at the end and store it flat. The spray must be removed with its own solvent.

Your stencil work should be protected with a coat of matt, satin or gloss varnish, as appropriate.

USING MORE THAN ONE COLOUR

By following a few guidelines, stencilling in two or more colours will give beautiful results.

It is important that the stencil be left in place until all colours are applied. When painting each colour, use masking tape to mask off the areas where other colours will appear. The instructions (on page 11) for stencilling also apply to the other stencils in this book.

FLOORS

Floors need a little more explanation than walls, but they are easier to deal with than walls or ceilings as you have both hands free. Floors should be sanded smooth — by a professional sander if possible. He will hammer in loose nails and fill in nail head holes and other defects. The floor should be given two good oil-based undercoats after it has been thoroughly vacuumed and gone over with a *tack* rag which you can buy from a hardware shop.

Each coat of paint will take 24-48 hours to dry, so the room should be kept locked to avoid cats, dogs and children leaving little traces. Undercoating is followed by two coats, also oil-based, of your chosen background colour. You can buy special fast-drying floor paints which are excellent. You now have a good surface to work on. One last vacuuming and thorough going over with your tack rag and you are ready to stencil.

If you are making a repeating design all over a floor you lay out your work using chalked string in the same way as for a wall. If you are using a diamond or chequerboard design, two lines taken from the corners and crossing in the middle will give you the centre.

When painting the floor there are two golden rules. 1. Cover your hair completely as some hairs always drop into the wet paint. (If you find hairs on the floor while it is still wet, you can remove them with sticky tape wrapped around your index finger by using a light dabbing motion.) 2. Don't get trapped! Start in the far corner and paint your way out of the room towards the door. If the floor is made of boards, paint along the line of the floor boards. If you are putting down another covering in sections (craftboard for example) these can be undercoated before laying.

When your design is finished and completely dry you will need to varnish it. Follow the directions on the can and allow the correct drying time. You will now have a hard-wearing floor which can be simply mopped clean with a damp sponge. If the surface starts to wear, give it a light sanding and put on a few more coats of varnish.

It is particularly important to strain paint and varnish as the cans *always* end up with bits of dirt and grit in them; they are transferred from the floor to the brush no matter how carefully you have cleaned and dusted the floor.

FURNITURE

Furniture should be in sound condition, so repair where necessary. Fill all holes and sand with 'wet and dry', whether it is painted or clean wood, till the piece is smooth all over. Preparation is the most important part of a well painted piece of furniture.

Use two oil-based coats of undercoat and two *thin* coats of the chosen main colour. Use paint thinly, otherwise you will get dribbles. If the worst happens and you do get a paint dribble, remove it carefully with a scalpel when dry and sand smooth. Using water, sand lightly in-between the colour coats with fine 'wet and dry' using a circular motion. Clean off the *mud* that appears during this process with hot soapy water and dry thoroughly. When quite dry you can begin stencilling. Choose your stencil design to suit the style of the piece of furniture and make sure it is in good proportion to the size of the surface on which you are working — neither too large nor too small.

Once your stencilling is dry — up to 48 hours — protect it with several coats of satin or gloss varnish, whichever is appropriate to the appearance of the piece. I recommend between three and five coats, lightly sanded with 'wet and dry' between coats. This will ensure that you end up with a piece of furniture which is silky smooth to the touch and which can be further protected with wax polish.

FABRIC

Stencilling on fabric is essentially the same as for the surfaces already described, but there are a few differences as you will see.

Materials

Absorbent paper (don't use old newspaper as it can leave dirty marks)
Fabric dyes or paints
Stencil brushes
Drawing board on flat printing table
Drawing pins
Fabric
Metallic spray

If you are using stencil board you will have to waterproof your stencil by giving it several coats of gold metallic spray paint on both sides. This is because fabric dyes and paints are water soluble and will make the board disintegrate. If you use an acrylic or plastic stencil it will already be waterproof.

New fabric should be washed to remove any dressing and then ironed and pinned out flat. Fabric or garments should be pinned or taped firmly to a hard, flat surface on top of several layers of absorbent paper to absorb excess dye or paint and to reduce blotching. Remember to put paper *inside* garments as well, otherwise you will have two printed layers — front and back!

Stencil with your brush exactly for the oil paint method and leave to dry. Treat according to the instructions on the fabric paint. After stencilling, lampshades, curtains and blinds can be sprayed with 'Scotchguard' to protect them.

You might also like to stencil a design onto tapestry canvas and embroider as usual. This way you can create entire room schemes.

PAPER

There are so many things you can make out of stencils on paper — lampshades, book covers, drawer liners, for example. Try stencilling on some of those lovely rag papers, vellum or Japanese handmade papers. Try making your own wallpaper by printing on rolls of lining paper.

Materials

Stencil brushes
Artists watercolours or gouache colours, poster colours, inks etc.
Any kind of absorbent paper, parchment, vellum etc.
Metallic spray paint

For this stencilling use the brush as for the previous methods, or use matt paint from a can, or ink using a mouth spray.

First of all, waterproof your stencil by spraying both sides of it with several layers of metallic spray paint and leave to dry. Pin out the rolls or sheets of paper, or tape the extreme edges, padding underneath with newsprint.

Secure your stencil with pins or tape, then stencil in the usual way, holding your brush like a pen and using a pouncing movement with a very little paint on the brush. The work can be protected with a spray of clear varnish especially designed to make paper moisture- and dirt-proof.

If you want to stencil a lampshade it is best to find some good quality card, parchment or vellum and cut to shape, stencilling while flat and assembling the shade later. Ready-made lampshades can be stencilled by using spray paint and plenty of masking tape, or spray with coloured ink and an artist's mouth spray, again mask surrounding areas well. Protect your design with clear paper varnish and it will wipe clean. You can also make lampshades without paint by cutting the shade out like a large stencil and lining it inside with different coloured paper or cloth. This gives an interesting effect when the light shines through.

Happy stencilling!

NOTES

1. John Seymour, *Forgotten Household Crafts* (Angus & Robertson, Sydney, 1987).
2. Ibid.
3. Acetate is transparent and waterproof and is a good material to use when the stencil is simple or when you have an extensive project, such as stencilling an entire room. It will last throughout your project, unlike a weaker material such as cardboard. Some people do not like to use acetate because it is expensive and because it can be difficult to cut smoothly. You can use acrylic sheet instead of acetate. Although acrylic sheet is less transparent, it is more pliable so it's easier to cut around corners.

FURTHER READING

General

1. Clark, K., *The Nude* (Penguin, Middlesex, 1960).
2. de Dampierre, F., *The Best of Painted Furniture* (Weidenfeld & Nicolson, London, 1987).
3. Furneaux Jordan, R., *Western Architecture* (World of Art series, Thames & Hudson, London, 1969).
4. Gombrich, E.H., *The Story of Art* (Phaidon, Oxford, new edition 1989).
5. Jones, O., *The Grammar of Ornament* (Bestseller Publications, London, 1988).
6. *Sturgis' Illustrated Dictionary of Architecture and Building* (Dover, New York, 1989).
7. *Historical Ornament. A Pictorial Archive* (Dover, New York, 1976).

Greek and Roman

1. Masson, G., *A Concise History of Republican Rome* (Thames & Hudson, London, 1913).
2. Strong, D., *The Classical World* (Paul Hamlyn, London, 1965).
3. Summerson, J., *The Classical Language of Architecture* (World of Art series, Thames & Hudson, London, 1980).

Baroque and Rococo

1. Bazin, G., *Baroque and Rococo* (World of Art series, Thames & Hudson, London, 1964).
2. *Baroque and Rococo — Architecture and Decor* (Portland House, New York, 1988).

Victorian

1. Banham, J., Porter, J. and Macdonald, S., *Victorian Interior Design* (Cassell, London, 1991).
2. Daly, C., *Interior Design Motifs of the 19th Century* (Crescent, New York, 1988).
3. Laver, J., *Victoriana* (Ward Lock & Co, London, 1966).
4. Naylor, G., *The Arts and Crafts Movement* (Trefoil, London, 1971).

Art Nouveau

1. Reade, B., *Art Nouveau and Alphonse Mucha* (H.M. Stationery Office, London, 1963).
2. Tahara, K., *Images of Fin-de-Siecle* (Kodanska International, Tokyo, 1988).

Art Deco

1. Arwas, V., *Art Deco* (Academy Editions, London, 1980).
2. Calloway, S., *Art Deco – Interior and Panel Designs* (Crescent, New York, 1988).
3. Hillier, B., *Art Deco* (The Herbert Press, London, 1985).

Paint Finishes

1. Bennell, J., *Masterstrokes* (Hutchinson, Australia, 1988).
2. Drucker, M. and Finkelstein, P., *Recipes for Surfaces* (Cassell, London, 1990).
3. O'Neil, I., *The Art of the Painted Finish for Furniture and Decoration* (William Morrow, 1971).
4. Radford, P., *Surfaces and Finishes* (Macmillan, London, 1984).
5. Sloane, A. and Gwynn, K., *The Complete Book of Decorative Paint Finishes* (Century, 1988).
6. Spencer, S., *The Art of Marbling* (Greenhouse, Victoria, 1988).

GREEK AND MINOAN

(5th – 1st Centuries BC and 3000 – 1100 BC)

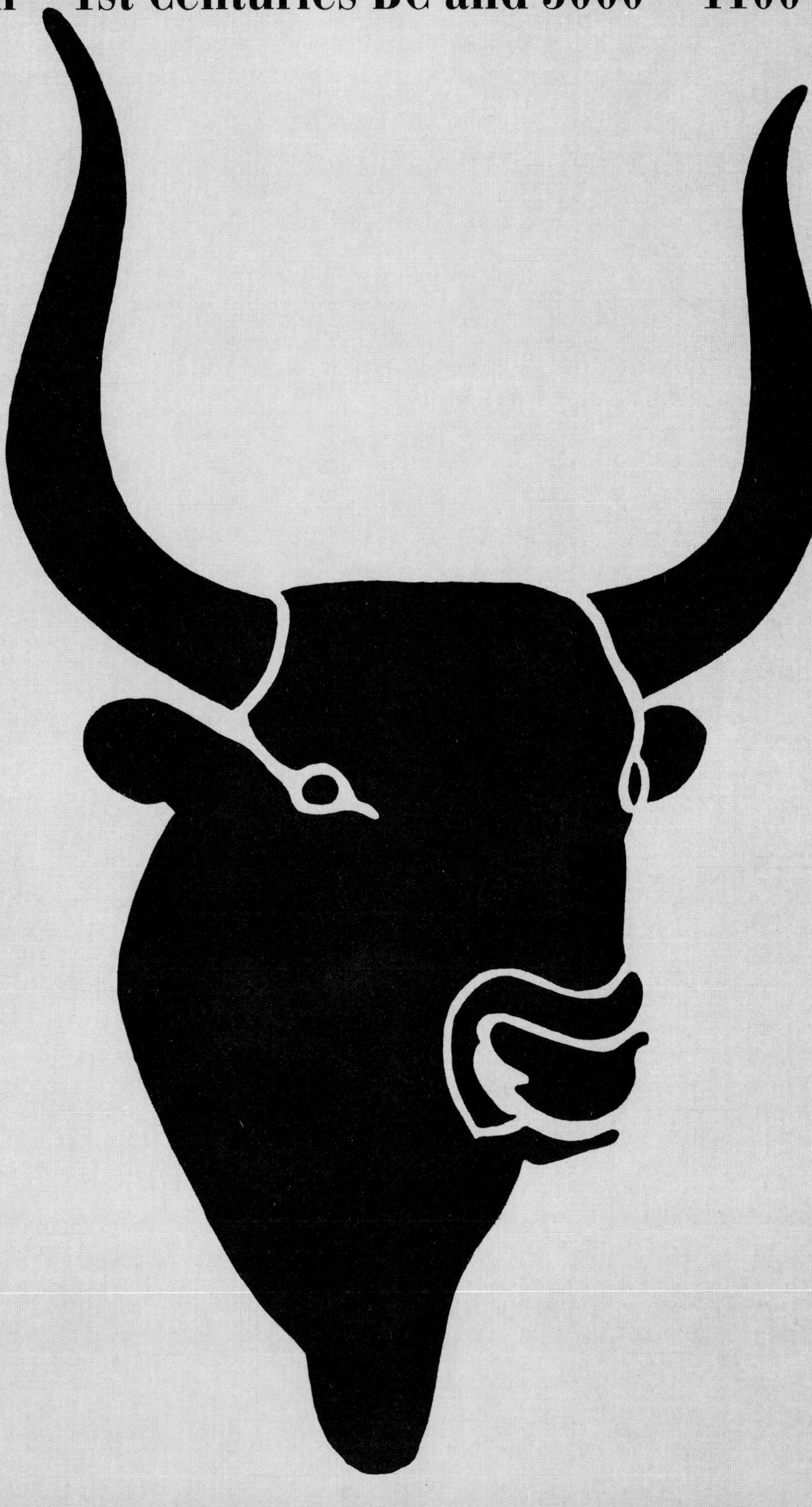

GREEK AND MINOAN

It is no exaggeration to say that the arts and architecture of ancient Greece have had a longer lasting and more profound effect upon Western civilisation than those of any other cultural group.

Architecture until quite recently has shown an amazing indebtedness to the Greeks. Just look down any main street in any large town and the Greek influence can be seen clearly in the construction and decoration of grand public buildings such as town halls, libraries and banks.

Greek art and architecture is often described as classical, a term that generally describes anything relating to the ancient Greek and Roman world, but has also come to signify emotional restraint and regularity of form.The Greeks managed to combine intellect with passion and nature with mathematics, which is why their designs are so potent and long-lasting.

The stencils in this section are based on the three main kinds of decoration which have come down to us, namely architectural, sculptural, and brush drawn decoration preserved mostly on pottery.

When dealing with architectural stencils it is most effective if the main shapes are sponged with, say, two similar shades of paint to give the impression of stonework with shadows laid on top in an even-coloured darker shade. Where a line or curve has to be arrested because a tie is necessary, the gap in the design must be filled in after the stencil is removed from the wall. Marbling the main shapes can also be very effective, stencilling in this case being done with a stippling glaze and veins brush drawn finely while the stencil is in position. Veins can also be drawn in with oil pastel and glazed over to complete. Grisaille work — that is work in a few shades of grey on a neutral stone colour — can look wonderfully effective and produce a formal elegance and coolness.

Greek painted decoration made much use of natural motifs such as vines, ivy, bayleaves, Greek key design, scrolls and dots, the latter being made with the end of a paint brush. I suggest that you do the same thing, as cutting dots is very difficult with a scalpel. If you do want dots cut out of the stencils, use a knitting needle or bodkin (for making broderie anglaise), and sand off any projections at the back to keep the stencils flat.

When you consider decorating a room in the Greek manner, give due consideration to the correct colour scheme. We think of Greek architecture as plain stone or marble but it was colourfully decorated when new. And Greek pottery is coloured mainly in the terracottas, earths and ochre colours of the available clays with the addition of white and black.

I have included stencils which will make splendid schemes for formal areas, where muted stone colours can be used with great success and simple trompe l'oeil effects achieved. The stencils of formal decorative bands should be coloured in the earth colours already mentioned if used in conjunction with the architectural stencils. They are suitable for wall decoration, picture rails, dados and chair rails, and for floors and ceilings.

The more lively stencils based on animals and plants are less formal in their effects and would be fun to use in spa rooms, around indoor pools or gyms, bathrooms, patios and any outdoor area.

MINOAN

I have included Minoan designs with Greek because I have to confess to being especially fond of the amazing ability of the Minoans to combine a love of life with a superb sense of what is decorative. Crete was also very influential in the development of early Greece and injected much sophistication into the Mediterranean at an early date.

Minoan designs, although simplified and abstracted, remained much closer to nature and less formal than Greek ones and their use of colour seems to have been brighter and more vivid, with reds, greens, yellows and blues included, no doubt under the influence of Egypt with whom they shared early historical ties. But there are none of the frozen qualities of Egyptian art in Minoan painting. Minoan art is bursting with life and movement, full of references to plants, animals and above all the sea and the creatures in it. It is sophisticated but unselfconscious, and not a bit pompous or grand. I'm sure the Minoans were a rather frivolous, fun-seeking lot, if their paintings are anything to go by. The pleasures of the senses are very evident in their work.

Some themes persist in Minoan art and I have made stencils of those I feel are most attractive to modern eyes. The lily is almost a Minoan signature — so extensively was it used in decorating buildings and pottery. Irises and rushes were also used and birds, fish, dolphins, shells and octopus and all references to the bull cult were very popular. Some of the Minoans' favourite designs would not be so attractive or desirable to us — squids, octopus and jelly fish for example — so the choice of motifs in this section has been based on what still has decorative force today and can be most usefully translated and transposed into the stencil medium. Delight is, I think, the main experience we feel when looking at Minoan art.

These Minoan stencils would happily go anywhere that's sunny, light-hearted and associated with the sea. They can be used in conjunction with painted finishes such as distressed fresco, sponging and primitive marbling.

Anthemion. A flat decorative band very common in Greek decoration. This stencil uses one colour.

Fifth Century BC Ionic capital and column developed from Temple on the Illissus, Athens.(Greek).

Shaft: every 25-30 cm (10-12 inches) the fluting should stop for a join which will run horizontally across the shaft. You may get a similar fluted effect by using masking tape the whole length of the shaft to get continuous fluting – that way you can also achieve the tapered effect a real column should have. Real columns taper towards the top and are also slightly curved outwards (entasis).

Base: if you enlarge this stencil greatly you may find you have to make new ties to strengthen it at (a) and (b) parallel to the central tie. Spaces left by the tie should be filled in once the stencil has been removed from the wall.

This whole column would look terrific if sponged with two soft stone colours, one on top of the other, or marbled in white faux marbre. Once the stencil is printed, the spaces left behind by the ties must be carefully sponged, or otherwise filled in, to give a more realistic effect.

A stencil of this size and complexity must be stuck to the wall during stencilling with a proprietary spray adhesive to help hold it in place. But please read the instructions on the can as these products can be dangerous.

ABOVE: Beading and bead and reel moulding. (Greek). The lower stencils show moulding using two stencils to achieve a trompe l'oeil effect. First trace and print the whole design in light stone. Then trace out the darker colour and print the second stencil in dark stone over the first colour.

BELOW: Egg and dart design using two stencils to suggest three dimensions. (Greek). For the first stencil the *whole* design is painted in grey (tracing out both black and grey parts). Print the black areas second on top of the grey print.

BOTTOM: Egg and dart ornament taken from the Erectheum, Athens. (Greek). This stencil uses one colour. After stencilling, the white gaps are filled in with a small brush using a stippling motion.

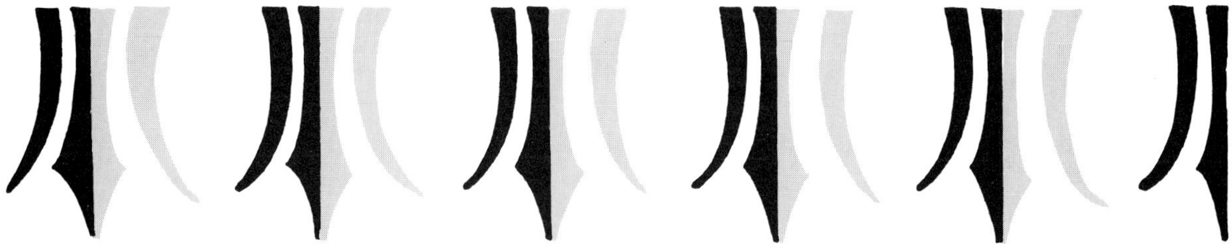

Lion motif taken from a Greek drinking vessel found at Chios, and now in the Louvre, Paris.

Apollo and Artemis in the battle of gods and men. (Greek). Archeological Museum, Delphi. The eyes must be painted separately.

Stencil based on the *Todi Ares*, a bronze statue in the Vatican Museum. (Greek).

Eagle with fish. (Minoan). Taken from a vase in the Candia Museum, Crete.

Eagle from Laconian cup in the
Louvre, Paris. (Greek).

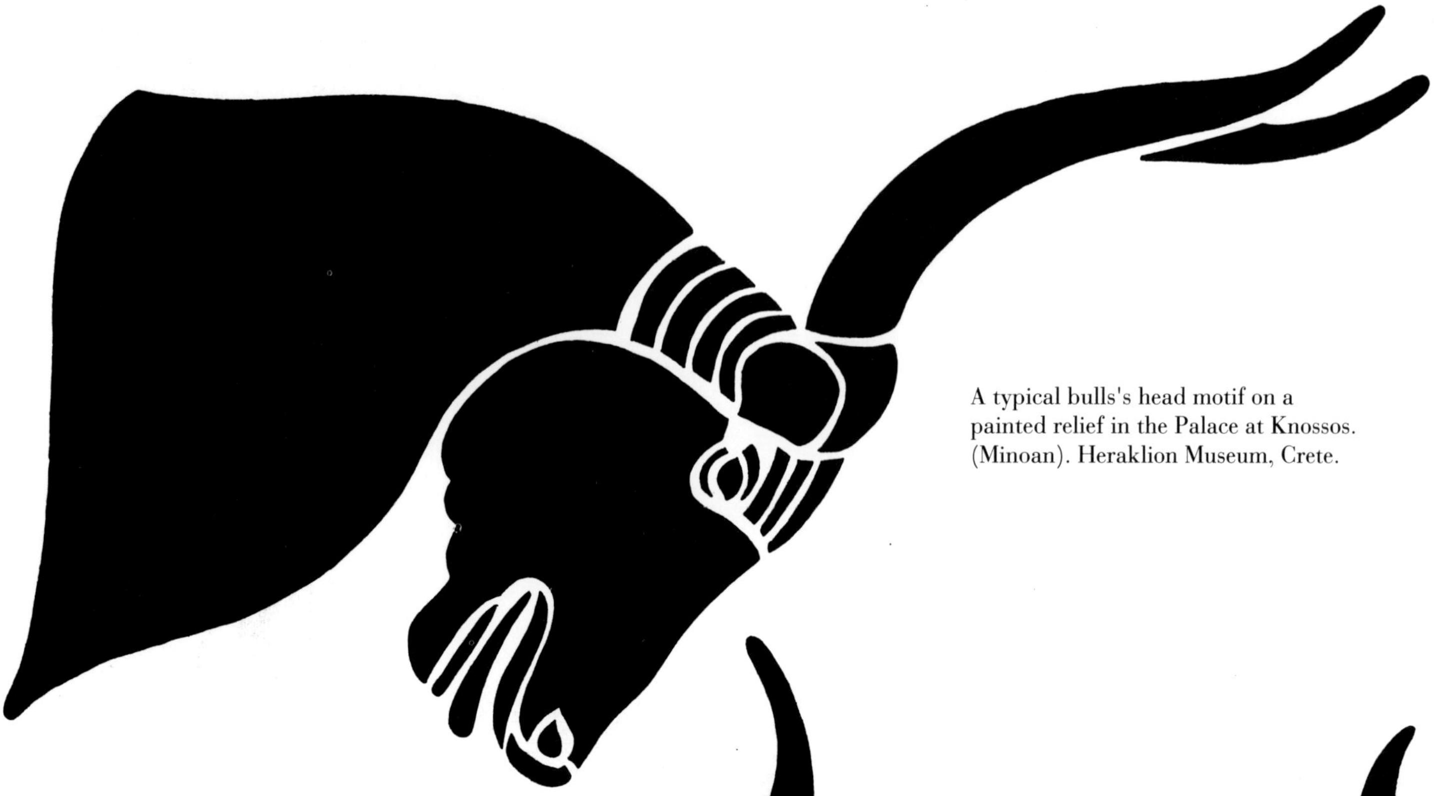

A typical bulls's head motif on a painted relief in the Palace at Knossos. (Minoan). Heraklion Museum, Crete.

This design is based on a drinking vessel or rhyton found at Knossos. (Minoan).

Frieze of flying fish based on a fresco by a Cretan artist found at the palace of Phylakopi. (Minoan). The main colours are blue, black and yellow with soft green daubed onto the background to suggest weeds. A sponged background, or distressed fresco treatment on the wall would make this stencil look terrific.
The eyes need to be dotted in after stencilling.

BELOW: Stencil based on a wall painting in the Palace at Knossos.(Minoan).

A design based on a Medusa head found in the ante chamber of the tomb of Philip of Macedon at Vergina. (Greek).

FACING PAGE TOP: Anthemion (Greek)

BOTTOM: Anthemion using three colours and three stencils to give a trompe l'oeil effect. (Greek). The first stencil traces the *whole* design in the lightest colour. The second stencil is the mid colour printed on top. The third stencil is the darkest colour printed last.

From a fragment of wall decoration. (Minoan). Heraklion Museum, Crete. White lilies with dark green leaves on a wall decorated in stepped bands of pale green on a dark pink upper wall. The white lily motif was a favourite of the Minoans.

ROMAN

(2nd Century BC – 4th Century AD)

ROMAN

I suppose when one thinks of Rome one thinks of might, brute strength, colossal engineering works and huge civic buildings, certainly not of religion, art and philosophy as one would of the Greeks, to whom beauty and aesthetics always came first.

Much as the Romans admired Greek culture, their own culture was much more sturdy, coarse and state orientated. And lots of their decoration reflects the militaristic nature of Roman life.

Roman architecture borrowed heavily from the Greeks, using the basic post and lintel construction of the classical Greek temple and in-filling with arches to give what we think of as a typically Roman look, such as is seen on the Colosseum. In comparison to the elegance of Greek temples it seems heavy, massive and repetitious.

The Romans preferred the opulent Corinthian order of architecture characterised by columns with capitals of carved acanthus leaves. In their hands the style became more complex and florid, and they designed a new order based on it, the Composite. They used the acanthus a great deal in scrolls and borders — heavily carved, often fussy and overdone so that buildings had an almost encrusted quality. In contrast to the Greeks, the Romans produced very robust, massive and opulent forms, sometimes bordering on vulgarity. More Hollywood than Hollywood you might say. Pomp, display and public spectacle were very important to them; hence their triumphal arches and the straight wide roads that run under them. And of course every Roman building always seems to have a massive inscription somewhere — lettering played a decorative part in their architecture.

So much for the public face of Rome. Within the enclosing walls of their villas the private face of art was a much less serious affair if the remains of Pompeii and Herculaneum are anything to go by. House decorations of great charm and skill and really quite modern appeal have been preserved in the ruins of these towns. There are many attractive wall paintings which show sacred rites, erotica, trompe l'oeil scenes, marbling, flowery tracery and scenes from everyday life.

Colours were many and various, based on available pigments — black, white, red earth colours, browny-greens and yellows predominate. It is hard to say looking at ruins just how bright the original colours would have been; however, I feel that the Romans and the Victorians had a lot in common in this area and shared a love of gaudy colour.

In the following designs I have tried to suggest all of the qualities which we think of as Roman, both formal and informal, and the symbols they used. Compare the Roman eagle to the one in the Folk Art section, for example. Unfortunately some things like mosaics, which are so typically Roman, I have only been able to touch upon. I think these designs prove that some Roman ideas and designs are just as potent as those of the Greeks and have travelled down the centuries quite successfully.

A senator wearing the toga. Stencils based on statues like this one look very good in niches, arches or equally spaced around a room, especially in a stone or bronze colour.

ABOVE: A one colour trompe l'oeil stencil to suggest a carved border. The design is taken from the sarcophagus (stone or marble coffin) of Scipio Barbatus, Vatican, Rome. The breaks in the horizontal lines at (x) and (z) should be filled in after stencilling.

LEFT AND FACING PAGE: Borders from houses at Pompeii. Black with purplish red on terracotta, and black with orangey-red are two usual colour arrangements.

LEFT: Mosaic band taken from a floor at Pompeii. To look really effective, each of the strands in the rope could be stencilled a different colour, say black, yellow and white, with black outer bands.

Corinthian capital.

Corinthian capital from the interior of the Pantheon, in Rome.

TOP: Design taken from a relief celebrating one of Sulla's victories. Roman eagle clutching a thunderbolt in its talons and a palm frond in its beak, flanked by winged victories. Museo dei Conservatori, Rome.

CENTRE: Design based on a pavement edging.

BOTTOM: A continuous border of scrolled acanthus leaves.

ABOVE: Dancers in a Dionysian rite from an inlaid wall panel.

BELOW: Fragment of carved frieze, Forum of Trajan, Rome. In two colours to give trompe l'oeil effect.

LEFT: Bust. Use balanced on a column or in a niche as a decorative element. Rows of busts are quite effective, too, around a classically decorated room. The first colour printed should be pale.
The second colour printed should be dark.

BELOW: Vine leaf garland from a house known as Villa Farnesina at Pompeii circa 20 BC. This was painted at regular intervals upon panels separated by vertical coloured bands.

RENAISSANCE

(Late 15th – 16th Century)

RENAISSANCE

The classical revival called the Renaissance was a rebirth of interest in everything Roman. The painted arches and flamboyant soaring rib-vaults of the Gothic style gave way to the calm rhythm of orderly columns, round arches, roundels and beautifully carved and decorated pilasters.

The Renaissance began in Italy because Roman civilisation was everywhere still in evidence. Buildings were still standing and antiquities constantly being dug up. Interest was also revived by classical scholars fleeing from the Turkish occupation in 1453 of the ancient capital of the Holy Roman Empire, Constantinople (modern Istanbul).

Professor Nicolas Pevsner said 'The Renaissance was for the merchants of Florence, bankers to the Kings of Europe'. And certainly the princes of the Church, themselves secularised, were equalled in status by merchant bankers like the Medici who were patrons of everything cultured in Florence, using their money to build palaces and villas and great monuments to themselves, rather than to God. Thus, unlike the ecclesiastical Gothic movement, the Renaissance was an essentially secular one. Man replaced God as the measure of all things, humanism winning over Catholicism.

The great achievement of the Renaissance was the establishment of the grammar of antiquity as a universal discipline. The five architectural orders — Doric, Ionic, Corinthian, Tuscan and Composite — were defined by Serlio, Vignola and Palladio. Mathematics and nature were integrated with immense skill, creativity and verve.

The Renaissance also provided us with some of the finest painters and sculptors of Western art, in particular the three greats — Michelangelo, Leonardo and Raphael.

The circle and half circle are of great significance to Renaissance architecture and design. For the Greeks the simple form of post and lintel was paramount. To the Romans the arch reigned supreme, triumphal or arcaded. The Italian Renaissance was dependent on the perfect form of the circle which, being perfect, had divine connotations. Other important decorative forms included designs based on plants, animals, masks, human bodies, classical myths — as found in Roman decoration — with the grotesque playing an important part.

However, Renaissance artists were also working within the Christian tradition, and thus Christian imagery was found alongside classical themes. It was an uncomfortable liaison often leading to some strange results.

When choosing colour for these stencils, I would point you in the direction of the great painters mentioned — rich golds, browns, and greens would all be appropriate. You can also look at majolica (pottery glazed with bright yellows, blues, greens and oranges) of the period and at Luca della Robbia ceramics. But the best thing to do is enter into the spirit of the style in which you are decorating.

I have tried to choose designs based on the very best art of the period to give some of the overall flavour. Essentially the Renaissance is a curious mixture of energy, genius, confidence and discipline combined with immense good taste and artistic virtuosity — a very exciting time for the arts of man.

Putti based on figures from *The Nymph Galatea* by Raphael, Villa Farnesina, Rome. Features and bowstrings can be painted in after stencilling.

FOLLOWING PAGES: Classically simple Italian sixteenth century alphabet based on incised Roman alphabets. Very easy to read in comparison to the florid style shown below, and therefore most suitable for public inscription. Note that 'I' and 'J' and 'U' and 'V' are the same in this alphabet. By Serlio, from *Alphabets Old and New* by Lewis F. Day (B.T. Batsford Ltd, 1910).

A B C
D E F
G H I
K L M

NOP

QRS

TVW

XYZ

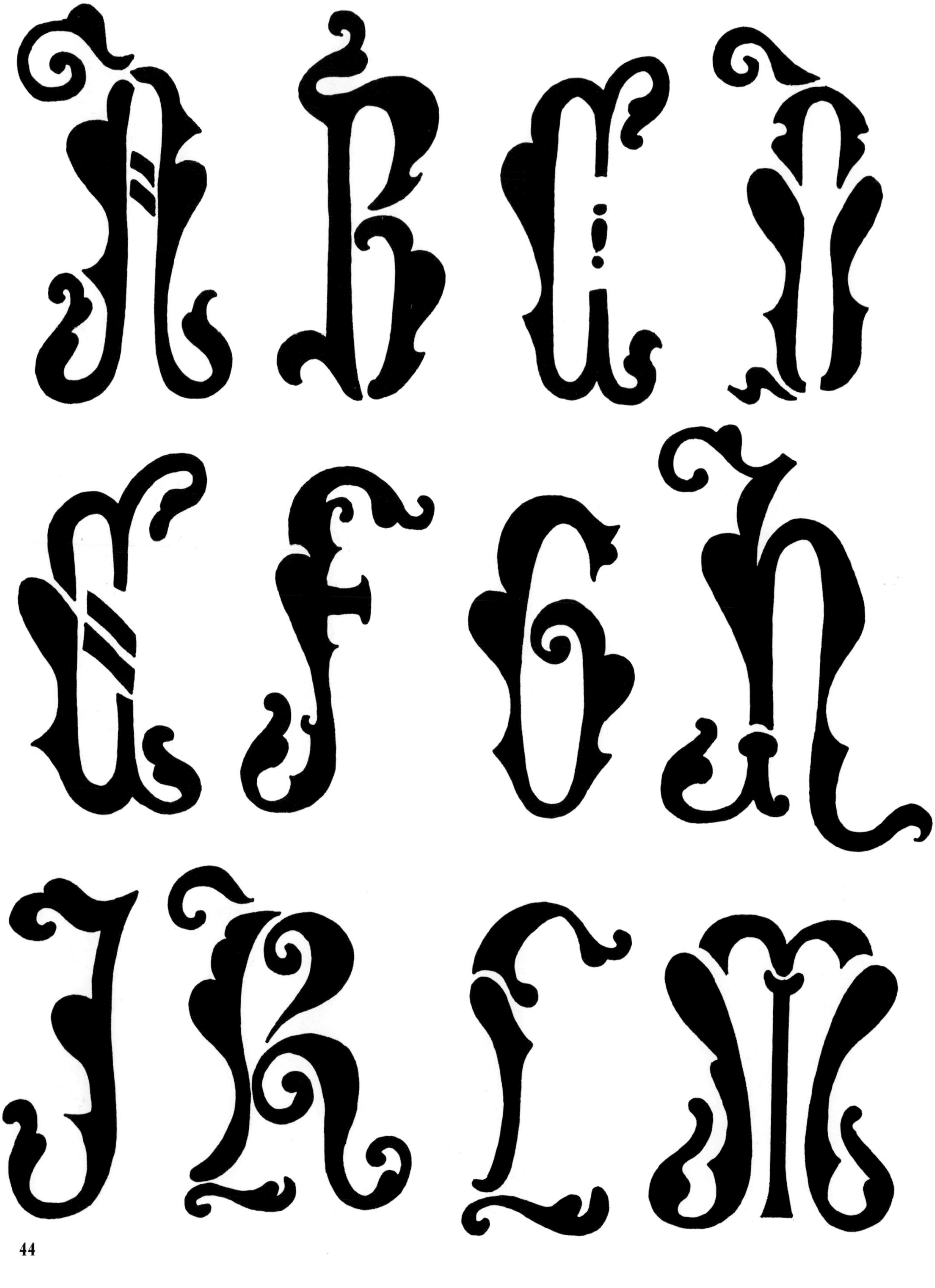

PREVIOUS PAGES: An alphabet derived from an Italian one of 1570 in the florid style by C.F.Cresci. This a fanciful fretted style suitable for cut metal, inlay on painting, on furniture or interior work. Note that 'I' and 'J' and 'U' and 'V' are the same in this alphabet and there is no 'W'. These alphabets show the two extremes of the Renaissance – elegant simplicity on one hand, ornate freely flowing natural forms on the other.

RIGHT AND FACING PAGE: Grotesque heads, flambeaux (burning torches), baskets of fruit, meandering tracery, bows and flowers were all favourite motifs.

ABOVE: Meandering tracery with grotesque head.

BELOW: A repeating band of oak leaves and acorns based on the wreath worn by one of the five grotesque heads in a drawing in the Royal Library, at Windsor Castle, England.

ABOVE: Arabesque taken from Leonardo's *Profile of a Warrior in Armour*, 1486, British Museum, London.

RIGHT: Decorative chalice design.

ABOVE: Design based on a carved panel in a church in Pavia, Italy.

BELOW: Decorative basket of fruit.

FACING PAGE: Angel, bird, cornucopia and dolphin all combine in this Italian panel to give a rather grotesque effect. Paint the angel's features after stencilling.

A grotesque window from the Palazzo Zuccari in Rome, designed by F. Zuccari, 1592.

Mercury by Giovanni da Bologna, Bargello, Florence, 1567.

A scallop shell and a swag of leaves and flowers – developed from part of the altar in *The Annunciation* by Leonardo in the Uffizi gallery, Florence. The flower centres can be spotted in after stencilling with the tip of the handle of your paint brush.

BELOW: Based on an edging by Michelangelo from the Sistine Chapel ceiling, Rome.

BAROQUE AND ROCOCO

(Late 16th – 17th Century and 18th Century)

BAROQUE AND ROCOCO

Put most simply, Baroque refers to the post-Renaissance style which started in Italy and broke all the classical rules for art and architecture which the Renaissance had defined. It is irregular, informal, unexpected and, some might say, even vulgar or tasteless in its abandonment of classical traditions.

Baroque is very grand and is characterised by electrifying energy and a wonderful kind of masculine vigour. It is the counterblast to the Protestant Reformation and represents the resurgence of reformed Catholicism over humanism. Baroque art reflects a return to religious passion and ecstasy, great saints and miracles. In Catholic countries these themes were most powerfully expressed in churches and other ecclesiastic art. In Protestant countries the Baroque expressed itself mostly in secular buildings and ecclesiastic architecture was much more restrained. In Latin America Baroque is known as the Jesuit style, quite aptly.

The most characteristic shapes and motifs for Baroque are the sunburst often with clouds, the twisted corkscrew column made famous by the sculptor Bernini, trompe l'oeil scenes which 'opened up' walls and ceiling surfaces to let light in, as it were, coats of arms, escutcheons, scrolls, banners, urns, hunting trophies, musical instruments, stylised floral scrolls and putti. Colours were rich and strong.

By contrast, Rococo is a rather charming, feminine, frivolous and superficial decorative style which followed hard on the heels of Baroque and continued until the French Revolution and the new discipline of neoclassicism at the end of the eighteenth century. Rococo decorative effects can be found in pristine condition in hundreds of churches in Switzerland, Austria, Bavaria, Bohemia, and in all areas where Puritanism never really caught on.

Where Baroque is characterised by the extravagant expression of powerful emotion, Rococo is rather more superficial. It is sinuous, sexy and voluptuous, lavish and frankly decadent. There are lots of similarities in its forms and arabesques to Art Nouveau, as we shall see further on in this book. Compare the two capitals in this section and you will see the difference between Baroque and Rococo. The first still obeys some classical order. The second embodies every kind of excess!

Rococo art is characterised by incredibly complex meanders of stylised plant forms, with intervening panels often filled with net-like or scale-like decoration in gold, and every kind of 's' shape, whiplash, arabesque and curlicue you can imagine. Popular motifs included very small putti, angels, shells, crimped ribbon and seaweed bands and irregular flower swags some of which eventually take on a decidedly Chinese effect towards the end of the eighteenth century. Rococo colours are soft pastels trimmed with white or gold.

It is very difficult to design only fifteen pages of stencils based on the plethora of designs and images from these times, but I hope that the designs I have made for this section will at least hint at the richness and diversity of these two contrasting periods of decorative design and architecture.

English decorative urns used as finials.

Rococo alphabet. Note that 'I' and 'J' and 'U' and 'V' are the same in this alphabet and there is no 'W'.

ABOVE: Decorative urn on finial, based on decorative iron work in the Place Stanislas by Emanuel Here, Nancy, France, circa 1752. (Rococo).

FACING PAGE: Capital from Steinhausen by D. Zimmerman, circa 1728. (Rococo). Far removed from Greek or Roman styles, this is the extreme form of 'weddingcake' ornament. However, it can be very attractive in small doses.

RIGHT: Heart shaped ornament. (Rococo). Paint in the small lines after stencilling.

BELOW: Cherubs and clouds - another important Baroque and Rococo motif.

ABOVE: Border with hanging tassels – based on the cover over the baptismal font in the church at Ottobeuren, Bavaria, circa 1760. (Baroque).

BELOW: Cherubs, shell, ribbons and foliage – a typical Baroque arrangement for a panel. Taken from a marble inlay, St Catarina, Palermo, Italy.

RIGHT: Baroque sunburst.

BELOW: Sunburst with clouds – another favourite motif of the period. (Baroque).

ABOVE: Capital for a pilaster based on an acanthus – very different from the Greek and Roman treatment of the same motif. (Baroque). Taken from a gateway in Nancy, France, circa 1750s.
The spaces left by the ties must be painted on after the stencil is removed.

BELOW: Typical Rococo curlicues.

Pouting, pretty and pudgy – a typical Baroque putto. The smaller details can be added with a brush after stencilling.

FOLK

(17th, 18th and 19th Centuries)

FOLK

Folk art is the art of common people, the art of the man in the street, as opposed to the prince in the palace. It was the pop art of its day and is quite the opposite to the sophistication and grandeur of fine art, being simple and straightforward.

Folk art is typified by primary or gaudy colours used in a lively, spontaneous and naive way. Sometimes the drawing is crude and rambling, often without the underlying geometry of more sophisticated decoration. Folk art can be charming, vulgar or whimsical. It expresses itself through homely symbolism using hearts, ribbons, birds and crowns. Peacocks appear for marital devotion, doves for peace and biblical scenes and characters are frequent as is the tree of life theme. Cornucopia symbolise fertility and abundance, while tulips represent the Holy Trinity or perhaps even the Holy Family. Harvest festival symbols, the Bible and other familiar objects belonging to the daily life of a farmer or craftsman appear frequently on furniture, quilts and embroideries from the seventeenth, eighteenth and nineteenth centuries.

Folk art is by folk, for folk. It was executed and originated by journeymen (artisans) and humble joiners and craftsmen, some of whom, especially in America, were itinerants who wandered from town to town plying their trade painting rooms or pieces of furniture. Sometimes they painted curious and primitive versions of the decorations that graced lordly homes. The symbolism they used was understood by all; the willow tree for sorrow and death, the pineapple for hospitality, the outstretched hand for friendship.

In America different waves of craftsmen brought European symbols and fashions with them. English, German and Nordic traditions are very evident when looking at American folk art. But of course all of these styles ended up in the melting pot and a particularly American look came into its own using eagles, maize, the flag, morning glories and other non-European motifs.

Most ordinary furniture in Europe during the eighteenth and nineteenth centuries — especially that which was made of commonplace woods like pine, oak, ash and elm — was painted, sometimes because it wasn't particularly well jointed but usually because our ancestors liked colourfully decorated objects. Marriage beds, dowry chests and the family armoire (a large cabinet originally used for storing weapons) received a great deal of care and attention. In general nothing was left undecorated. Most pieces were painted first in a bright colour, different countries having different colour preferences. The Scandinavians used lots of blue, grey and green. The Austrians and Germans used more red, yellow and black.

The stencil designs that follow have been based on decorations found on artifacts from all over northern Europe and America, mostly from museums but I have used specific sources from other books and photos where indicated. This form of stencilling is particularly suited to country furniture and houses and an unpretentious life style. Beginners could start at this section with very good results.

Stencil based on an American watercolour, Pennsylvania, 1775. Features must be painted in by hand after stencilling. From drawings in *American Folk Art: Designs and Motifs for Artists and Craftspeople* by Joseph D'Addetta (Dover, New York, 1984).

The drapery with bows is circa 1837, birds and ribbon circa 1830, and the cornucopia taken from a Connecticut quilt of 1860. Based on drawings in *American Folk Art: Designs and Motifs for Artists and Craftspeople* by Joseph D'Addetta (Dover, New York, 1984).

Birds and flowers motif from a watercolour, Pennsylvania. Based on a drawing in *American Folk Art: Designs and Motifs for Artists and Craftspeople* by Joseph D'Addetta (Dover, New York, 1984).

BELOW: Motif based on a panel on an eighteenth century German desk.

ABOVE: Peacock. Make a separate stencil for the 'eyes' on the peacock's tail or hand paint them in later when you dot in the eye on his head.

ABOVE: Motif taken from an eighteenth century Swedish corner cupboard.

ABOVE: Peacock design.

BELOW: Border of acorns and leaves, a common English and American motif.

ABOVE: Decorative panel taken from an Austrian armoire, 1825.

RIGHT: Design based on a panel on an armoire from Alsace dated 1841, Salzburger Museum. Blackish-green and red on a deep cream ground.

RIGHT: Strawberries and harp motif based on an American quilt design motif, Maryland, 1845 from a drawing in *American Folk Art: Designs and Motifs for Artists and Craftspeople* by Joseph D'Addetta (Dover, New York, 1984).

Pear tree motif. Stencil based on an American painted wooden urn, Pennsylvania, 1861. From drawings in *American Folk Art: Designs and Motifs for Artists and Craftspeople* by Joseph D'Addetta (Dover, New York, 1984).

FACING PAGE TOP: Cornucopia motif from a stencil quilt, Boston, 1820. Based on drawings in *American Folk Art: Designs and Motifs for Artists and Craftspeople* by Joseph D'Addetta (Dover, New York, 1984).

BOTTOM: American eagle motif taken from a quilt, Connecticut, 1807. Based on designs in *American Folk Art: Designs and Motifs for Artists and Craftspeople* by Joseph D'Addetta (Dover, New York, 1984).

RIGHT: Motif taken from a Swedish cupboard signed Hans Wilstrom and dated 1793, Nordiska Museum, Stockholm. Orange, gold and green on a cream ground with blue-green body and surrounds to the panels.

LEFT: Flower basket based on eighteenth and nineteenth century motifs.

BELOW: This stencil is based on a panel taken from the Per Olaf Hallin cupboard from Vasterbotten, Sweden. It is now in the Nordiska Museet, Stockholm.

RIGHT: A wedding crown or two, hearts and floral wreaths would look very good on a marriage chest or bed head.

ABOVE: The pineapple is used in America to symbolise friendship and hospitality. It appears on quilts, cupboards and boxes in endless permutations.

RIGHT: Cornucopia – a typical American motif of the eighteenth and nineteenth centuries. Based on a quilt in the Shelburne Museum, Vermont, USA. The dots and lines on the pineapple should be hand painted after stencilling.

ABOVE: A merman to partner the mermaid on a chest or bedhead. Facial features and chest details can be painted in after stencilling.

RIGHT: Mermaid design based on similar eighteenth century designs from a marriage chest and particularly popular as a motif in America. Facial details and fins can be painted in after stencilling.

VICTORIAN

(1837 – 1901)

VICTORIAN

The very long reign of Queen Victoria covered a vast number of styles, from the very worst industrial design to the particularly attractive, designed by the members of the Arts and Crafts Movement and William Morris in the 1880s.

The origins of Victorian art and design elements are somewhat eclectic. The Victorians borrowed heavily from the Greeks and Romans, however, there was also a distinct and heavy bias towards the Gothic. As the Empire spread and Britain came in contact with other cultures and different kinds of art, even more influences occurred — particularly from the arts of India.

With the discovery of photography it became much easier to copy things for industrial purposes — straight onto printing plates — so design proliferated. Not that this technological advance was necessarily a good thing. Victorian taste in general was appalling; often fussy, encrusted, over coloured and vulgar. As Dickens said in his *Tale of Two Cities*, 'It was the best of times and the worst of times' from a design point of view.

In this section I have included examples of the best Victorian design — so it is biased. There are recurring themes. The tea rose, ivy, lily-of-the-valley, and forget-me-nots were probably the most popular plant motifs. Disembodied hands or feet, not to mention shoes and boots seem to pop up a lot. And there was almost a cult of death and mourning due to the expanding population and high infant mortality rate — the death of Prince Albert increased its intensity — so black was a very important colour in Victorian furniture fabrics and wallpaper. The invention of the new aniline dyes made colours much more intense, hard and garish which accounts for some of the bad taste. The Victorians excelled at sentimentality in design with lots of fat cherubs, small children, puppies and dogs. It is the beginning of the modern cult of what is described as 'cute'.

The Victorians' excessive use of ornament everywhere, on everything, eventually produced a counterswing that gave us Modernism and a complete lack of ornament on anything by the 1950s and 1960s. But in order to arrive at the totally undecorated look decorated design, as it were, made two last stands — Art Nouveau and Art Deco, the latter being the first truly modern style. These will be dealt with in later chapters.

ABOVE RIGHT: Decorative ribbon bows – a favourite motif.

BELOW: Small birds such as this finch are frequently seen in Victorian decoration. The eye can be painted in later.

BOTTOM: Ribbon and bow taken from a wallpaper design.

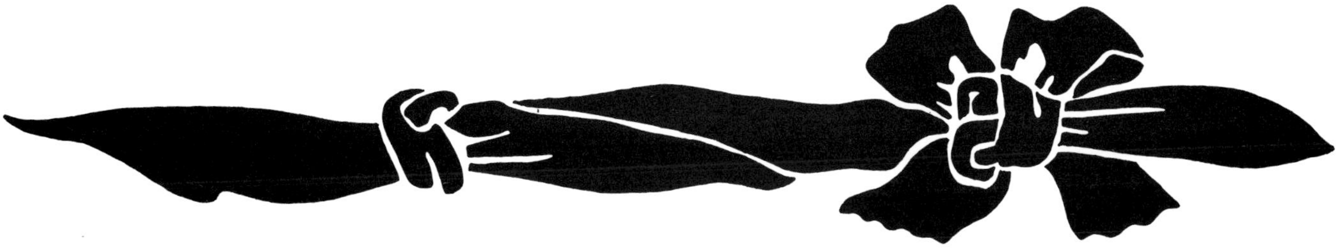

TOP: Border from an illustration in *Ornamental Design for Woven Fabrics* by C. Stephenson and F. Suddards (Methuen, London, 1897).

CENTRE: Ivy, a popular plant motif, creates this border. Stencil the dark areas in light green and the open leaves in dark green to get the most interesting effect.

BOTTOM: Chrysanthemum border based on a Victorian wallpaper design.

Stylised border.

Ceiling rose, 1860.
Fine lines can be painted in after stencilling.

ABOVE: Floral border based on illustrations in *Ornamental Design for Woven Fabrics* by C. Stephenson and F. Suddards (Methuen, London, 1897).

Design based on the crocus taken from *Ornamental Design for Woven Fabrics* by C. Stephenson and F. Suddards (Methuen, London, 1897).

ABOVE RIGHT: Free flowing plant forms create this typical spray design for a bracket on a cast-iron pub table.

BELOW: A lovely deep border of full blown tea roses taken from a late Victorian wallpaper by Laneway and Carpendel, 1898, American. Stencil the centres of the blooms deep pink/red and gradually shade off the petals towards the edge.

RIGHT: Typically sentimental, flowering motifs with the rose much in evidence.

BELOW: The tassels and cat's features must be painted in after stencilling.

China doll. Paint in the features after stencilling.

The Victorians were preoccupied with death and symbols like this one abound in their art and design. They also were very fond of veiled weeping women, ivy, wreaths and weeping willow trees.
Paint features after stencilling.

ART NOUVEAU

(1890 – 1914)

ART NOUVEAU

Art Nouveau is the last great romantic movement in art. It was a reaction to imitative, eclectic Victoriana and the coarse mass-produced monstrosities which filled Victorian houses.

Art Nouveau is linear in its expression, that is, its effect comes through line rather than colour or light. A perfect example of the style is the famous 1895 wall hanging by Herman Obrist, *Cyclamen.* It is known as The Whiplash because its curves are as vigorous and powerful as a cracking whip. Certainly it is very far removed from the reality of the plant it was based on.

Art Nouveau is typified by the use of curves, feminine forms, plant forms — always expressed in vigorous, rhythmical lines — and a return to greater clarity and simplicity. Art Nouveau style twists in stems, smoke, women's hair and peacock feathers. It twines in tendrils around upright stair rails and across wallpapers — all is movement in Art Nouveau. It often has a delicate, almost fairy-like quality. This is especially so in the book illustrations of Aubrey Beardsley and Walter Crane. Favourite motifs of Art Nouveau are peacocks and their feathers; nymph-like women with fantastic flowing hair; abstract, meandering, tense lines (usually found in wrought iron work); insects, butterflies — often with human bodies — and dragonflies; twining plants of every description; waves and foam.

In its asymmetry Art Nouveau bears some resemblance to that other feminine movement Rococo, where similar meandering plant forms are used. But Art Nouveau has more vigour, energy and movement than Rococo and is more forcefully decorative where Rococo often lapses into rather limp patterning.

Colours which typify Art Nouveau are the peacock colours — lustrous blues and greens — gold, orange, violet and the colours of precious stones like jade, chrysoprase, moon stones, opals, baroque pearls, and metals like bronze and pewter.

There are so many examples of wonderful Art Nouveau jewellery, illustrations, fabrics, wallpaper and furniture that it was very difficult to make a small selection. I have chosen designs which I felt captured the spirit of Art Nouveau.

It is a most decorative style and was resurrected with great success in the 1960s in association with the hippy movement, women's liberation and the general relaxation of rules. It has such vigour and beauty it will probably become fashionable again when modernism, post-modernism and nouveau brutalité have run their course.

A panel filled with the perfect features and flowing hair so typical of the Art Nouveau female ideal. This design is adapted from an Alphonse Mucha drawing, 1897, Victoria and Albert Museum, London.

RIGHT: Dandelion design based on the cover of *Studies in Plant Form and Design* by W. Midgley and A.E.V. Lille (Chapman & Hall, London, 1895).

BELOW: Ogee-shaped motif which can be used as an all over design, a border, or a single design.

Flower and bee design based on an enamelled brooch by C. Dessosiar for Fouquet, 1901.

Repeating borders based on a campanula and nasturtium from *Nature Drawing and Design*, Part II by Frank Steeley (G. W. Bacon & Co., London, 1903).

Two poppy borders adapted from drawings in *Nature Drawing and Design*, by Frank Steeley (G. W. Bacon & Co., London, 1903).

Design based on a statue of Lois Fuller, *Le jeu de L'Echarpe* by Agathon Leonard, 1900. A dancer at the Follies Bergere and subject of many Art Nouveau designs, here she is performing her famous scarf dance. She was the embodiment of the rhythm and verve of Art Nouveau.

ABOVE: Design based on a necklace by René Lalique.

BELOW: Border based on the Scarborough Lily from a design by A. E. V. Lille and W. Midgley, *Studies in Plant Form and Design* (Chapman & Hall, London, 1895).

Peacock feather — a favourite motif of the period. This one could be used as a border in conjunction with the same feather on a smaller scale dotted here and there as a 'sprig' at intervals over a wall. Purple, blue, green and gold are usual colours.

Flowering rush. Repeating vertical stripe design based on a drawing by W. Midgley, *Studies in Plant Form and Design* (Chapman & Hall, London, 1895).

ABCD
EFG
HIJKL
MNOP

Alphabet. Typically elongated lettering with pen-drawn, asymmetrical curves. Adapted from a design in *Alphabets Old and New* by Lewis F. Day (B. T. Batsford Ltd, 1910).

Three designs based on decorative motifs, designed by Otto Wagner from Karlsplatz Station, Vienna.

ART DECO

(1920s – 1940s)

ART DECO

Art Deco (decorative) is the first truly modern style. It is radical and unique, showing very little connection to traditional design of the past and seems very remote from late Victorian design which produced Art Nouveau.

Art Deco looks as though it is machine-made rather than hand-made. Often objects look like machines, rather than being related to anything natural such as plants or animals. The main shapes found in Art Deco are zig-zags, lightning bolts, pyramids, squares, diamonds and sunbursts. The general effect is abstract, mechanical, geometric and streamlined.

Art Deco sprang out of industrialisation — the Henry Ford assembly line idea. It was influenced by art movements such as Cubism with its reduction of natural forms into geometric planes, Italian Futurism with its celebration of the machine age, by the abstract artist Mondrian, and by the costume designs for the Ballet Russe, especially Diaghilev's 'Les Biches'. The discovery of Tutankhamen's tomb and its important finds also injected Egyptian influences into Art Deco design. However, the most important influence was the machine age itself — speed, motor cars and aeroplanes; everything shiny, new and modern. It was a city style for city slickers — and was the height of sophistication.

In the following stencil designs I have tried to incorporate all of these influences and present the correct flavour. The designs range from the purely abstract and angular to those based on popular themes of the day — deer ('Les Biches'), antelope, other streamlined animals like borzoi (a Russian deer hound) and greyhounds, and equally streamlined females cast in the glamorous Hollywood star image. We also encounter Amazons, Diana the Huntress and other images of female freedom and emancipation.

Art Deco colours were cream and gold, pastels (apricot and green in particular) often spattered with gold, lacquer colours (red and black) and metallic colours such as gold, silver and bronze. There were unusual and startling combinations like turquoise and orange. But it was, in the words of the famous song, a time of 'Anything Goes'.

Art Deco is above all a self conscious, glamorous style. It is what it says it is — art decorative. And it was during this period that the idea of having someone called an interior designer who organised colour schemes, furniture and gave a house a 'look' first came into being. Suddenly the house could be designed like a stage or film set — a place to be looked at first and lived in second.

So if you like drama, modernity and 'flash' effects this is a style worth trying in your home.

A stylised floral border – try it in oranges, yellows and greens. Based on a French vase design.

A border based on waves, sea spray and rising sun – typical of the period.

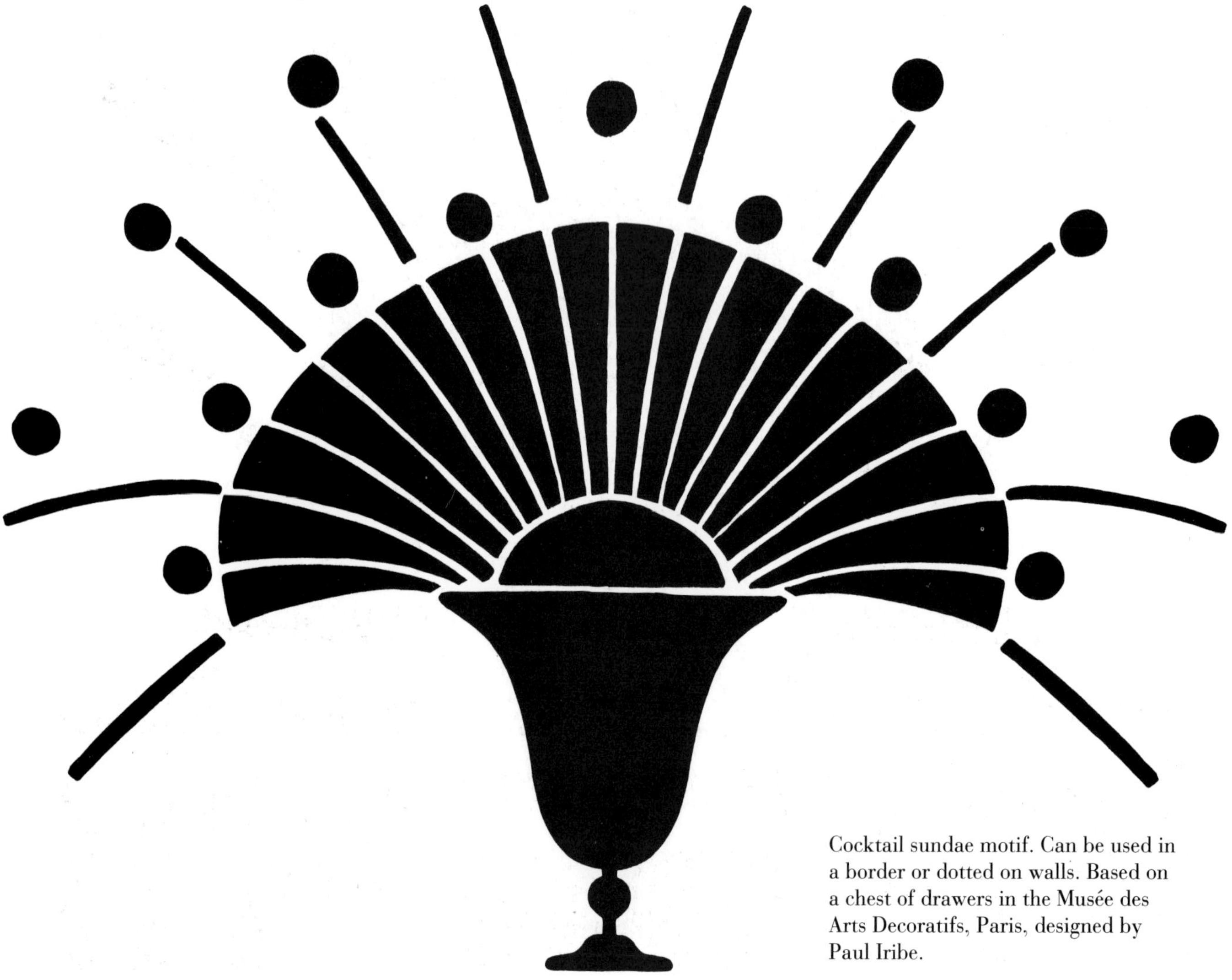

Cocktail sundae motif. Can be used in a border or dotted on walls. Based on a chest of drawers in the Musée des Arts Decoratifs, Paris, designed by Paul Iribe.

An interesting combination of a sunburst and a ziggurat (an ancient Sumerian type of temple) – two Art Deco motifs in one. Taken from a radiator grill.

Girl's head with 'sunburst' of hair.

BELOW: Cornucopia with tassels.

ABOVE AND RIGHT: Geometric borders taken from pottery of the era.

BOTTOM: Border showing how to turn corners. Taken from an original design in a house in Greenwich, Sydney.

A lean and elegant lady with a lean and elegant hound – typical motif. Taken from a moulded glass plaque circa 1925 by Marius Sabino. Paint in features and lead after stencilling.

FACING PAGE TOP: Design based on a metal screen by Edgar Brandt, 1920s.

FACING PAGE BOTTOM: Border with hind motif and sprays – typical of the period. Try this in two colours.

Based on a lamp design of a dancer holding two spheres (lights). Add small features after stencilling.

Stylised wreath of oranges, leaves and bows.

Amazon with her bow. Add the bowstring and eye with a fine brush after stencilling.

Two more examples of the ideal Art Deco female form. Both based on statues of the period. Add eyes and small details after stencilling.

Typically streamlined Art Deco animal forms. Add small lines and features after stencilling. Use them to make borders in simple rows or reverse and alternate them.

The 'boule' rose – a typical Art Deco/Art Nouveau motif based on a circle. This rose also appears in Art Nouveau designs by Rennie Mackintosh and others.

GLOSSARY

ACANTHUS — a carved ornament based on the leaves of the acanthus plant; a feature of Corinthian style columns.

ANTIQUING — the creation of the patina or sheen of antique objects. A common method is to apply different layers of colour and then partially remove them. Transparent glazes tinted with greys or browns can also create the effect.

ARABESQUE — a type of decoration featuring curved lines with intricate intertwining designs.

ARTS AND CRAFTS MOVEMENT — a Victorian movement led by William Morris, it sought to revive traditional craftsmanship and handicrafts.

CLASSICAL — this term has a number of meanings. Most commonly it is used to describe anything relating to, or characteristic of the civilisation of the ancient Greeks and Romans. However it is also used to describe a style of art or architecture characterised by emotional restraint and conservatism.

CORNUCOPIA — a representation of a horn overflowing with fruit, vegetables etc.

DADO — the lower part of an interior wall that is decorated differently from the upper. Dado rails originally defined this area and were designed to protect walls from the backs of chairs.

DIONYSIAN — Dionysus was the Greek god of wine, fruitfulness and vegetation and was worshipped in orgiastic rites.

DISTRESSING — achieving an appearance of age or excessive wear.

ESCUTCHEON — a heraldic shield.

FINIAL — a knob-like ornament, often in the form of a fleur-de-lis and appearing on the top of spires, pinnacles etc.

GLAZING — the effect of painting thin, almost transparent layers of colour over others to produce a washy or textured finish to the surface.

GOTHIC — refers to a style of art and architecture of the twelfth to sixteenth centuries.

HUMANISM — the rejection of religion in favour of belief in the advancement of humanity by its own efforts. Specifically, a cultural movement of the Renaissance based on classical studies.

LUCA DELLA ROBBIA — refers to glazed terracotta invented by Renaissance artist Luca della Robbia.

MARBLING — the technique of imitating marble in paint.

PILASTER — a shallow rectangular column attached to the face of a wall. It usually has a base and capital.

POST AND LINTEL — the simplest structural device, it consists of two posts spanned by a beam (lintel).

PUTTO — a representation of a small boy, cherub or cupid.

RELIEF — in sculpture, refers to forms or figures which project from a flat background.

ROLLED RAG — a technique for wall painting using a rolled or scrunched up rag which is pressed into a wet glaze.

ROUNDEL — a small circular window.

SPONGING — a method of creating a textured, dappled effect with a sponge dipped in paint.

STIPPLING — applying paint with a brush to give a speckled appearance.

SWASTIKA — a primitive religious symbol in the shape of a Greek cross, usually having the ends of the arms bent at right angles.

TROMPE L'OEIL — literally meaning 'a trick of the eye' this is a painting technique used to create an illusion of perspective and reality by the use of shadows and highlights.